A Little Bit of Everything

poetry by

Helen Minazza

Thank you to everyone who helped with the creation of A Little Bit of Everything. Without their support this book would not have been possible.

In particular … thank you Ben, Wendy, Steve R, Helen, Keri, Claire, Rowena, Scott, Lynsey, Adam, Lisa, Amy, Jen, Suzi and Steve P.

Copyright © Helen Minazza, 2014
All rights reserved

www.helenminazza.com

For my sister, Karen

Contents

Apparition	6
Listen	7
My Boys	8
Shadows	9
Pedestal of Light	10
Painting	11
97	12
Awakening	13
Pale in the Dark	14
Bubble	15
One Alone Stood	16
B4 11	17
Passion of Yours	18
Circus Chimp	19
Prisoner	20
In the Dark	22
The Burden You Bear	23
Lost in Meaning	24
Desperately Alone	25
The Student	26
False Pride	28
Dilapidated Daffodil	29
Unicorn	30
Questionable	31

Sleep, Reality, Death	32
Seconds	35
You to Me	36
The Heavens	39
Fate	40
Void	41
Free	42
Green Man	43
Valentine	44
Hale-Bopp	45
Winter	46
Have You Got Any Brown Sugar?	47
Hold Me	48
I Could Find You	49
Lamplight	50
Leaving Home	51
Operation	52
Take My Hand	53
The Back Seat of Life	54
The Messenger	55
Time	56
War	57
Together We Stand	58
Escapism	59
Table	60
Who Are You?	61

Apparition

The sun is low over the headland,
The sky a pattern of colours.
The stars begin to shine in the depths of the darkening heavens.
The salt in the air lingers on my lips.
A gentle wind blows and a lock of your hair is caught, dancing in the breeze.
Strains of music float on the night,
Confessions of undying love and eternal happiness, weave through the melodies.
I look to you and imagine tender kisses,
The gentle probing of your hands caressing my cheek, my neck, my chest.
Your touch soft, like the breeze that plays with your hair.
The darkness becomes deeper, you fade into the night.
The scent of you is all that remains … you are but an apparition of the wind,
Carried away on the breeze that brought you to me.
Once again I am alone.
Resting my chin upon my knees,
Hugging my knees to my chest,
As if to replace your presence.
I taste the salt on my lips.

Listen

Listen, listen.
For what are we listening?
Bells ringing,
Birds singing,
Shhh listen.
Hedgehogs scuttling,
Foxes foraging,
Listen, listen.
For what are we listening?
Owls hooting,
Humans shooting,
Listen, listen.
For what are we listening?
Shhh listen.
Silence.

My Boys

I never imagined I could feel so strongly,
It feels like all that had gone before was just playing at love.
The first moment I saw you, held your hand,
I felt such a depth of emotion I never thought I would feel.
Looking into your tiny face, half of which came from me,
The biggest fear I felt was that I would ruin you.
Your perfect innocence, unquestioning love,
Unspoiled by idiosyncrasies or prejudices.
I wanted to keep you perfect, looking out at the world with unjaded eyes.
Imprinting myself on you is inevitable, moulding you with my way of doing things.
I only hope that you keep in mind how special you are,
How unique and worthy of life.
There are people out there that will want to tear you down.
I hope I give you self-worth enough to combat them.
I love you both, my boys.

Shadows

All of the places I think of today,
Have all gone, corroded away.
Shells of memories and joys we made,
Now discordant where melody played.
Shadows walk through the past,
I see the traces they made last.
The path we trod is now so old,
The love and emotion now so cold.
I miss those times and familiar people,
My life has now entered a brand new season.

Pedestal of Light

I think of you all alone,
Helpless in the night.
Suspended above us all,
On a pedestal of light.

I want to reach for you, comfort you,
To tell you it's all right.
There you sit above us all,
On a pedestal of light.

Darkness is all around,
Suppressing the use of sight.
And there you sit above us all,
On a pedestal of light.

No one can compare,
Can beat your dizzying height.
Still you sit above us all,
On a pedestal of light.

The longing to be near,
The longing to set things right.
You're out of reach above us all,
On a pedestal of light.

Painting

Jump into a painting,
Dance the flows and eddies.
The wind sounds the rhythms,
The sea plays the melodies.
The paintbrush keeps time,
As you dance the flows and eddies.

Jump into a painting,
Sing to the depths and heights.
The mountains beat time eternal,
The valleys moan and hum in time.
The paintbrush conducts the chorus,
As you sing to the depths and heights.

Jump into a painting,
Recall your loves and losses.
The rolling fields pluck the heartstrings,
The drifting clouds dance for sorrows.
The paintbrush draws upon your memories,
As you recall your loves and losses.

97

97 people all sat in fancy pews.
Fluttering ties and tipsy bonnets all the saucy rage.
Tumbling down the aisle with acrobatic feats.
Thrilling quivering bottoms out of bottom polished seats.

Awakening

A deep darkness overflows,
No shapes, just perpetual darkness.
Can't move, don't want to move.
Fear, paralysing fear.
The dread of the unknown petrifies.
Eyes flick open, ears strain into the night.
A cold sweat breaks, shivering.
A scream, tears, light floods the room.
A deep, grown up voice caresses the ears,
Soothing, caring.
Lifted, helped, enveloped in love.
Tiredness takes over,
Eyes droop … going, going, gone.
A deep friendly darkness takes over.
A dreamless sleep, empty of all emotions,
But love and comfort always warm the heart.

Pale in the Dark

The darkness surrounds my body,
Friendly, forgiving darkness.
The pale skin and sensitive eyes,
Are borne of the darkness that is undeath.
I travel the streets soundless as a ghost.
I make my way around the sleeping city,
Prowling the deathly silent streets.
I smile at death.
I dance to the tunes of decadence.
A vessel of sustenance lies at my feet.
I smell the blood pounding through its heart,
This meal soon to be another unexplained death.
As I smile at the cold seclusion I am about to give,
Fangs grown into being.
Razor sharp, the glory of giving death,
Cold and beautiful like a black rose.
I raise the vessel to my lips,
I pierce the forgiving skin.
Euphoria flows through my body.
The life giving blood makes me feel alive,
Giving me borrowed time.
The stolen blood brings colour to my cheeks,
And vitality flows through my body.
I'm satisfied … for now.

Bubble

Sitting in a bubble,
The craziness locked outside.
People rush back and forth,
While I am in my bubble.
Warm, relaxed, serene, content,
Letting life pass me by for once.
Out of the crazy rat race,
Mellow, relaxed, serene, content.

One Alone Stood

One.
Alone, stood.
The brightening pre-dawn,
Silhouettes the tall imposing church.

One.
Alone, stood.
Hiding in the shadows of the church,
Skulks the form of a woman.

One.
Alone, stood.
A solitary bird sings greetings,
To the morning's risen sun.

One.
Alone, stood.
Gunshot rings clear in the cold,
The form falls to the ground in silence.

One.
Alone, stood.
Against Them.

B4 11

"Ring me before eleven."
Tonight eleven?
This morning eleven?
Before the very first eleven?
Rewind time to the very first eleven,
Watch time unravel, ruck like a ribbon.
A blue shiny ribbon,
Floating through the space-time continuum.
Very first eleven,
Ring, ring,
Oops no phones.
Before ever,
B4 11.

Passion of Yours

I feel a cold metal chill about my being,
A cold numbing shield about my mind.
Restricted as I am,
I still feel the purple energy that is your passion,
Burning deep in your centre.

The fire of my being burns through my veins,
The knowledge of your passion weakens me.
Restricted as I am,
I can still see the pain that is your passion,
Burning deep in your eyes.

I now know what you desire of me,
The power to command my life is yours.
Bound by design,
I see the madness that is your passion,
Burning in your face.

You strip me emotion by emotion,
My dignity trampled in the sands.
Standing by will alone,
You see my power buried within,
Defiance burning in my eyes.

Circus Chimp

Life is worth much more than this,
Yet here I sit day in day out,
Trampled by stereotypes and thugs that know no better.
Here I sit reading the same script like a parrot on a
    perch,
Like a performing dog I'm told to jump through hoops,
"Roll over, play dead".

Prisoner

A deep reverential fear,
Floods from the unknown.
Minutes change to hours,
Hours turn to days,
As I wait in fear for what the jury says.

Relinquished the power I once held,
Locked forever in a cell of time.
Mountains quake, floods threaten the land.
The jury votes,
I cannot stay the hand.

Voices cry out to me for help,
I hear them pleading, crying, dying.
Part of my torment is to watch and listen,
A tear caught,
On my face does glisten.

Powerless and defenceless,
I tread my path.
I bear the brunt of all anguish,
Unable to protect myself from despair.
This is the burden I have to bear.

Time passes me by,
Hours turn to days,
And in their turn, days to years.
Tortured as I look on helpless.

In the Dark

I scream a scream that nobody hears,
And my voice takes flight at the darkness.
I continue to search for love and light,
My voice still flees the darkness.
I shout, I moan, I scream, I call,
And yet I'm still surrounded by madness.
So help me please,
Don't leave me here,
Screaming a scream,
That nobody hears.

Author's comment – I think this should be read with a Scottish accent – that's how it sounds in my head.

The Burden You Bear

You gaze away,
Buried in deep emotions.
The bustle of family,
Masks your pain.
You come to the present,
To answer a question,
Or vaguely make a statement.
It is all a masquerade.
You don't fool me,
You're miles away, carrying a burden alone.
You don't need to be,
All you have to do is ask me.
I'll share your burden,
Hold you, guide you,
Share my world and security with you.
You no longer have to …
Gaze away,
Buried in deep emotions.

Lost in Meaning

Writing letters,
Creating meaningless words.
Empty vowels,
Hollow consonants.
Never quite writing,
Exactly what I mean.

Desperately Alone

I see you standing desperately alone,
In the shade of a tree at one …
With nature.

Serene, relaxed still desperately alone,
Something is missing, something …
Is lost.

You need someone by your side,
Look to me, I will relax you with my tide …
Of love and care.

I see you,
Desperately alone, gazing into the distance at one …
With nature.

What do you see?
Would you share it with me? Would you still be …
Desperately alone?

The Student

The sky reflects the ground,
A perpetual dark cold mass.
The standing stones, Earth's own flesh, in a circle stood,
Yielding the voice of the past to those who would listen.
A low moaning hum takes shape in the night.
It becomes stronger, separate voices that weave in and
    out of each other.
The songs of the wretched,
The songs of the rich,
The songs of the evil,
The songs of the good,
Of dryads, of druids,
Of centurions, of animals,
That in the woodland surrounding live and congregate.
A ghostly figure neither dryad nor druid,
Wanders between the stones, listening to the rising
    cacophony.
Mixed emotions rise to the night,
The love, fear, hate, rejoicing of every being,
That passed between those magicked stones.
Making no noise, the spectre like figure glides to the
    centre of mystery.
She listens to the histories flowing in the air,
The end to darkness, the beginning of enlightenment.

As the sun rises again, the songs and histories cease.
The figure wakes from a dream,
Knowing now what she must do.

False Pride

The inability to understand how you fit in the small picture,
For the big picture no one understands.
There are those that think they know,
And theirs is a false knowledge.

Dilapidated Daffodil

Dilapidated daffodil,
Lying on the table,
Subject of my suspicion.
What do you mean?
Are you a drunkard's gift?
Or a gift of a man trapped in a relationship?
Or simply a gift of friendship?
Dilapidated daffodil,
Lying on the table,
You are the subject of my suspicion.

Unicorn

The moon shines,
Radiant in the midnight depths.
Pin pricks of light reveal the stars,
Bathing the clearing in a cold, enhancing brilliance.
The serene stream mirrors the moon's eerie
    incandescence,
Resembling molten silver.
A majestic beast enters the clearing,
Stopping at the edge of the silver stream.
She surveys the woodland area,
And stoops to drink,
Pausing now and again, startled at every sound.
A single white horn rises from the beasts head,
The unicorn, for that is what this wild gentle animal is,
Shines so bright.
She emanates a pure aura,
That dissipates to the sky around her,
Adding beauty and strength to the moon and stars.
Her eyes are a soft liquid brown, caring and maternal,
The eyes of a mother and a lover.
She stands still and proud,
Before she enters the forest and disappears forever.

Questionable

If I were to answer any question,
What would it be?
If I could hold all the answers to all the questions for just one second,
Which question would I answer?
But if I knew all the answers to all the questions,
Shouldn't the question be ...
Which question would I leave unanswered?

Sleep, Reality, Death

I sit bolt upright woken by an indistinguishable sound.
The blackness around me folds into never ending shapes,
As the silence roars in my ears.
Unseen entities fly towards my face,
Stopping just inches from my unseeing eyes.
The denizens of the night whoop and scream,
Telling my unhearing ears of countless deaths.
I lay back down, my heart seems to be pounding through my chest,
As I imagine things tamer than those flying around my bed.
I force sleep into me, willing it to take over, ordering it to lead me elsewhere.
I impose my will, making it wash over me, touching every part of my body,
Forcing it into my mouth, between my legs and through my toes.
Sleep … the mantle that has become my body … my lover.

I sit bolt upright woken by an indistinguishable sound,
The blackness around me folds into never ending
 shapes.
The silence roars in my ears,
As unseen entities fly towards my face,
Stopping just inches from my unseeing eyes.
The denizens of the night whoop and scream,
Telling my susceptible ears of countless deaths.
I lay back down, my heart being ripped from my chest,
As I remember all but briefly the tales I was told as a
 child.
While I watch the denizens devour my heart,
I close my eyes and I know ...

I sit bolt upright woken by a sound,
The blackness is broken by flashing lights.
The noises in my ears roar,
As unseen entities push my prone body,
Upon an unreal fantasy.
The denizens of the light inform me of O.D.
I lay back, sinking through layers and wrappings of
 cotton wool.
The darkness around me folds into never ending shapes,
These shapes familiar,
And as the silent roaring abates I know the mantle that is
 my lover ... sleep,
Will never be broken again ...

I sit bolt upright ...

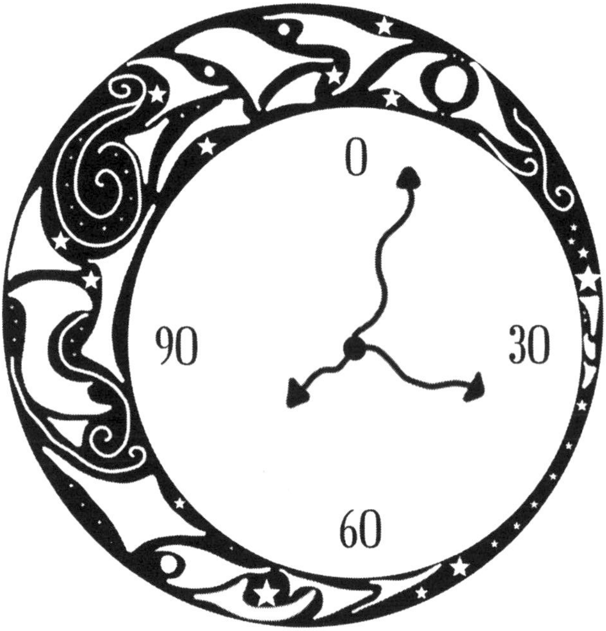
0
30
60
90

Seconds

Tick, tock,
Goes the clock.
Each second passing,
Bringing me closer to my death,
To my last breath.

You to Me

You to me are the earth,
A mountain of strength when I become weak.
Without you I would fall,
Deep and long into the abyss of unfeeling.

You to me are a breath of fresh air,
You breathe life into me when I flag.
Without you I would die,
Suffocated in this world of uncaring.

You to me are the waters of this world,
Carrying away worries and pain.
Without you I would break,
Buried in sorrows and misery.

You to me are the sunlight,
Warming me to the heart.
Without you I would pale,
Unable to conquer despair.

You to me are a shining beacon,
I am drawn unerringly to your light.
Without you I am nothing,
But a moth searching in the night.

You to me are a way of life,
I need, want, love you.
Without you I would cease to exist,
Only a faint memory on a breeze.

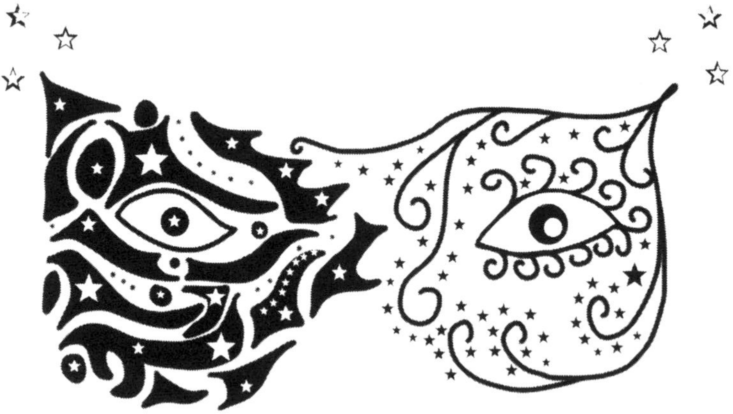

The Heavens

When the cold winds blow and Selene sings,
The clouds surround the moon adding a distant aura.
The stars, in a private masque waltz, dance to the
    eternal beat of the universe,
And the Earth spins on through the age old dance of
    survival.

Fate

Before the dawn of time,
As fate was preordained.
Alone in the dark, I sat waiting,
Waiting for the love I have yet to share.
An unknown face shines in my visions,
The features blurred, unreal,
Unknown to me.
And yet I know this is the man I will love …
The man I have yet to meet.

Void

The space between,
This and the next,
Is an empty one.
Nothing belongs here,
Not you, nor me.
Some try to fill,
Some try to expand.
They have no right,
To fill this void.

Free

As I close my eyes,
I pray for just one moment to forget who I am.
As I close my eyes,
I become as insubstantial as an autumn breeze.
As I close my eyes,
I learn to soar and swoop, taught by the birds
    themselves.
As I close my eyes,
I become an insignificant drop of newly formed dew.
As I close my eyes,
I melt into the earth and feel the life within.
As I close my eyes,
I become one with the slow pounding heartbeat of
    Mother Earth.
As I close my eyes,
My pain dissolves,
Drawn out by the hands of love.

Green Man

Patterns contrived by nature,
Discrepancies caused by man.
Point a steady arrowhead,
To the magic about to unwind.
The emptiness of a shadow,
Describes the shape of loss.
To refill the moment of desire,
The immortal must be lost.
Naked my body now stands,
The loss now almost a whole.
Ripples contrived by nature,
Shake the foundations of man.
Time expands through me,
Following the age old course.
We are now immortal,
The Earth no longer a source.

Valentine

Words cannot describe,
The feelings I have inside.
The burning in my heart,
Spreading to each and every part.
I love you,
I know it's true.
Be mine,
Be my Valentine.

Hale-Bopp

Fear of the unknown,
Embodied in a comet.
The tail of misery,
Follows closely.

Dreams of the future,
Embodied in a comet.
The tail of hopes,
Follows closely.

Fond reminiscence,
Embodied in a comet.
The tail of forgetfulness,
Follows closely.

The comet embodies,
So much, who can say,
What it meant then,
And what today?

Author's comment – if you didn't already know, Hale-Bopp is a comet that passes by every 4,000 years or so.

Winter

I watch the couples,
Walking by,
Holding hands,
I heave a sigh.

As the snow glistens,
On the ground,
Him and her,
Make their rounds.

I feel so lonely,
As they walk by,
Holding hands,
I heave a sigh.

Have You Got Any Brown Sugar?

Have you got any brown sugar?
Crystals that are brown and sweet,
To put in coffee,
Or to nibble neat.
When did they happen?
What are they for?
I'll tell you what, we need so much more!
Crunch, crunch,
Chew, chew,
You know that's not good for you!
But then again … have you got any brown sugar?

Hold Me

Hold me close,
Hold me near,
Into me you must peer.

Through my eyes,
You will see,
My heart, my soul, my real me.

Take your time,
To find me,
Hold me close then you will see.

I can love,
I can care,
Hold me close, take me there.

I Could Find You

If you were a bird flying in a flock of many,
Without hesitation I could see you flow with grace and style.
If you were a flower in a field of many,
I could sense you, searching out your heavenly fragrance.
Would I be lost to you if I were surrounded,
Unseen by your searching eyes?
If you were one in a choir of voices,
I could find your unique timbre within the harmonies of others.
If I were but a cloud in the sky,
Could you take my insubstantial being and hold me to your heart?

Lamplight

Standing under lamplight,
Waiting for it to dim.
Dreading the darkness,
It's coming from within.

Light is about to end,
Beginning the darkest reign.
It drags me down,
The never ending hole of pain.

Standing in the lamplight,
Each moment slipping fast.
It's all a game we play,
Future, present, past.

Standing under lamplight,
There's not long now.
The game is about to end,
The question on our lips is how?

Leaving Home

They came today, to take me away.
Where am I going? Where am I led?
They pull me along, amongst a throng.
So many people all in one place,
One of them picked up the pace.
Mummy and Daddy have all gone,
Have I been naughty for far too long?
I want them back, I love them dearly.
Where am I now anyway?
I want to be at home, now, today.
What is this room we're all in?
Don't shut the door the dark is scary.
What's that smell? Have they let loose all of Hell?
I can't breathe, I'm beginning to choke.
Are we all bad?
Is this what Jew means?

Operation

Am I worthy?
The gift is life.
Another has died,
They raise the knife.

Slice open my chest,
Peel back my skin.
Look at my heart,
That's beating within.

Hold my heart,
Pounding today.
My life's in your hands,
Don't throw it away.

Take My Hand

Take my hand,
Pretend for me,
I am not alone,
And you are free.

Take my hand,
As we walk the beach,
You feel so close,
To be out of reach.

Take my hand,
Hold me near,
Comfort me,
My love, my dear.

Take my hand,
As you took my heart,
Time draws near,
It's time to part.

The Back Seat of Life

Sitting in the back seat,
Watching life pass me by.
Scared to take control,
Afraid to grab the wheel.
I've got to take a risk,
There's always the chance of knockback.
"No pain, no gain", what do they know?
Taking courage in both hands,
Going ahead, grabbing the future in hope.
It will be all right … won't it?

The Messenger

This insubstantial being,
Spreads news.
The fleet footed being,
The Messenger.

No news is unworthy,
No terrain too rough.
He'll always get through,
The Messenger.

This being is invincible,
This being is tough.
Spread the word?
Use the Messenger.

Time

Time, what is time?
Does it go on and on?
Does it ever stop,
Or can you travel through it?

Time, what is time?
Is it like an endless pit?
Is it like a tuneless melody,
You can't get out of your head?

Time, what is time?
One hour can pass like ten years,
Two hours like two minutes.
Time, what is time?

War

Arms wide open,
Waiting … forever.
Empty sockets filled with love.
Hoping … you will be back.
The wordless mouth screaming for your return,
The tongue taken while you were gone.
Back flayed open by uncaring killers.
Needing your healing touch,
On hands and knees begging the Gods for your safe return.
Unconditional love pours from the prostrate body,
Not knowing the betrayal you committed.

Together We Stand

The craggy tops,
Reach for the sky,
Snow alights on the peaks.

The slow moving river,
Almost a mirror,
Reflects the indigo sky.

Serene at peace,
Together we stand,
Soaking up the vista.

The smell of pines,
Dance on the breeze,
Delicately tickling our senses.

The breeze has a chill,
Winter is coming,
We snuggle together for warmth.

With sticks in hand,
We race to the bridge,
Never too old for Pooh sticks.

Escapism

Drive along a long straight road,
Radio blaring favourite songs.
The sunshine almost blinding,
The open window providing,
A buffeting tunnel of wind.
A heady feeling of freedom flows through me,
As I light an accompanying cig,
To smoke my way to the sunset and beyond.

Table

I sat on my own,
All alone,
At a table,
With Clark Gable.
Drinking wine,
Feeling fine,
I punched a bloke,
Dealing coke.
I nicked his stuff,
And had a puff.
Feeling fine,
Drinking wine,
With Clark Gable,
At a table.
I'm all alone,
On my own.

Who Are You?

I don't know what your name is,
But I do know where you be.
Every time you think of love,
I hope you think of me.

Author's comment – please read in your best Cornish accent!

Thank you for reading

A Little Bit of Everything

www.helenminazza.com

Made in the USA
Charleston, SC
15 January 2015